Also by Lillian Hellman

PLAYS

THE CHILDREN'S HOUR (1934)

DAYS TO COME (1936)

THE LITTLE FOXES (1939)

WATCH ON THE RHINE (1941)

THE SEARCHING WIND (1944)

ANOTHER PART OF THE FOREST (1947)

MONTSERRAT (*An adaptation,* 1950)

THE AUTUMN GARDEN (1951)

THE LARK (*An adaptation,* 1956)

CANDIDE (*An operetta,* 1957)

TOYS IN THE ATTIC (1960)

MY MOTHER, MY FATHER AND ME (*An adaptation,* 1963)

THE COLLECTED PLAYS (1972)

MEMOIRS

AN UNFINISHED WOMAN (1969)

PENTIMENTO (1973)

SCOUNDREL TIME (1976)

THREE (*The collected memoirs, with new
commentaries by the author,* 1979)

EDITOR OF

THE SELECTED LETTERS OF ANTON CHEKHOV (1955)

THE BIG KNOCKOVER: SELECTED STORIES AND SHORT
NOVELS OF DASHIELL HAMMETT (1966)

Maybe

Maybe

a story by

LILLIAN HELLMAN

Little, Brown and Company — Boston–Toronto

FIRST EDITION

Library of Congress Catalog Card Number 80-11324

MV

Designed by Susan Windheim

*Published simultaneously in Canada
by Little, Brown & Company (Canada) Limited*

PRINTED IN THE UNITED STATES OF AMERICA

For
Ephraim London
and
Richard de Combray

Maybe

It was always with Sarah this way and that way all over the place, or maybe I never saw enough to understand. At a few points I know what happened, but there's a good deal I don't, because of time or because I didn't much care.

It's not easy. But not much is easy because as one grows older, one realizes how little one knows about any relationship, or even about oneself.

I don't even know if Sarah is dead, but I am fairly sure she was alive two years ago because I think I saw her come into the lobby of the St. Francis Hotel in San Francisco and go to the reception desk.

But was it Sarah? My eyesight was getting bad even then and I cannot be sure. As I moved toward the woman I thought was Sarah, I did hear the voice— Sarah had a strange way of speaking, as if words were not good enough or too much trouble. The possible Sarah did see me and the possible Sarah smiled at somebody back of me and moved away. A man stepped in front of me and by the time I got to the exotic, dark young clerk and asked the name of the lady who preceded the intruder, she said she didn't know who I meant.

I went to the house phones, asked for Mrs. Sarah Cameron, the last name I knew her by, which, of course, might not be the name she had now, but the phone operator, in the time it takes for them to forget what name you asked for, came back to say Mrs. Camp was not registered. It didn't matter: I was already sorry I had asked. What, after all these years, would we have said to each other?

And "all these years" meant nothing, anyway: we had never known each other really and, while some of her life had been deposited with me, I had good reason to think that much of what I heard was not true and, even when it was, there was something extra, vague, unthought out, maybe a half-nonsense reason I was being told it. I don't mean that she meant to use or profit from me: certainly not. I mean that each time I received a small bundle of the life, it was if she or her husband or someone had chosen me only because I was passing by or happened to be sitting next to them in the kind of small restaurant where you chat if you are alone, and sometimes even when you are not, with the man or woman sitting next to you.

Because, I think, a restaurant is where and how Sarah and I first met, although she always said we met at an anniversary party *The New Yorker* magazine gave in its early years. And she may be right: I do have a vague memory of a party but, when I asked people who worked on the magazine if they remembered it, they all said no, except Wolcott Gibbs who said there had been such a party, but he had never heard of Sarah. But of course she always thought she had met people at parties because she was always dropping in on them.

One of the strangest things about heavy drinkers, me among them, in those days—God knows it was also true of Gibbs—is that much that seems clear to you as you drink, in sober periods will never seem clear again, because of course it never was. Places, in particular: *The New Yorker* party or the Fourth Republic restaurant on the Rue Saint-Germain des Prés. It was all like that, anyway. But I am sure that the first or the third or the fifth meeting was in that restaurant because I remember Sarah, who was alone at the next table, asking me if she could help with the waitress who couldn't understand my patois New Orleans French. (Later, when I became a regular customer, the owner and the waitress, who was his mistress, and his mother who was not his mother, all used to congratulate me on the fluency of what they called my Marseilles French.) I cannot be sure that Sarah and I talked much that first night in the restaurant, but certainly we talked the next week or so when I came in with my husband. She had a small baby propped on her table. I remember the baby because he was long and very white. She said the baby's name was Isaac but he was called Som and he didn't like Paris. We left her in the restaurant after she was joined by a man and a young girl of about thirteen. The baby spat at the girl who spat back.

My husband said, "Odd. She isn't a beauty, but she looks like Garbo."

That was right, she did look like Garbo, but I think she was beautiful only when she didn't speak or smile. Then something else happened to the face: it was as if it had never been designed to move and when it did, then everything, mouth, nose, whole head, became too large. I thought that every time I saw her afterward. But what is afterward when you can't remember the times or the places of yesterday? I do, of course, remember many things about Sarah, but often what I do think I know does not fit what I heard from her or from other people when they talked about her.

Like everybody, I guess, I have had people wander in and out of my life who think they mean more to me than they do. They believe you have thought about them more than you have. It isn't always that they just want to feel important: it's some kind of mysterious misunderstanding that often puzzles and sometimes burdens you. In Sarah's case I don't think she cared what she meant to anybody.

From my point of view she was a kind of interesting drop-in and that never makes for sharp memories or much feeling. Her first husband, Carter Cameron, once said to me many years later, "It's not a question of life or people with Sarah. She has no interest in tomorrow because she has no interest in yesterday. It comes down to hours."

I said, "How much of her do *you* remember?"

"Only at first," he said, "and then partly because of my son. He has so much of the same thing now, only, only" — he touched my hair — "only nasty and that was never Sarah."

I had heard a little about Som through the years, and once, when he was at Princeton, he called me to say he was in trouble, could he come and see me? I postponed that meeting for a week or two and was then called by a man who said he was Som's friend and Som was holed up in the Royalton Hotel, couldn't get out because he couldn't pay his bill, couldn't go out, anyway, because he had hocked all his clothes and it was cold in March. I went around to the Royalton about an hour later, but either somebody had rescued Som or he had skipped.

A few weeks later I received a box of candied ginger from him with a note that said, "Don't run when you can stroll. Som Cameron."

I told Ferry Dixon about the ginger the next time she came to New York from Detroit. Ferry and Sarah had gone to Foxcroft together, had been close friends, or whatever you are on horses. At the dinner with Ferry and her heir-to-a-fortune husband, she got drunk very fast, or had been drinking before we met, and her husband certainly had been drinking. We were dining in "21," which, of course, dates and places Ferry and the millionaire, and immediately he ordered caviar, the best in the world, the rich kid said, and then fell asleep for a good ten minutes.

After I told Ferry about the ginger, asked about Sarah, she pointed to her dozing husband and said, "That's what I got for marrying money. I deserve what I got, is what you're thinking."

There is nobody so impatient with drunks as an ex-alcoholic, and that is what I was by then. And anyway how mixed up trivial things get when you come to know how little you cared about the passing people, should have known it, and not seen them again after the drinking years.

The boredom of that dinner was not easy because I knew Ferry was going to repeat whatever she was saying until she had a soothing answer or a fight. So

I decided to hell with it, and drummed out melodies on the table. The third time she said some form of you're sitting there thinking I deserved what I got, I said I wasn't thinking about anything except maybe some oysters after the caviar and that was strange because oysters didn't often taste good anymore, not after New Orleans or France, but I kept hoping for the best and ordered them, anyway. Didn't she think that was the only way to live? Hope? Just hope?

"You believe he's what I deserve. You wouldn't have married for money," said Ferry.

"Nobody with money ever asked me," I said, going as far as I was willing to go.

"What about Albert?"

"Alexander was his name and he was so poor that I think he courted me, or whatever the hell he was doing, in order to eat dinner at our house twice a week. My mother liked him because he had a soft voice, and, anyway, somebody took him away from me, thank God."

"Who?"

"I don't remember and I don't know and don't care."

"I don't believe that," Ferry said. "Every woman always cares about things like that. Shall I tell you who took him away?"

"Ferry, let it die with you," I said. "I want some oysters."

Ferry nudged the dozer who came to, smiling, and ordered oysters for everybody and a good bottle of wine and a couple of double martinis for himself.

Ferry said, "I think there's something nuts in remembering one thing and forgetting what you want to."

"O.K.," I said, "think what you like."

There was a good reason for my wanting to forget Alex. He had been a tall thin young man of twenty-three when I was nineteen, gentle, just out of college and on his way to a Ph.D., not sure if he wanted to paint or write, with the nicest voice and the quietest manner of any young man I had ever met.

He had been the first man I had ever slept with and the first time, like most, was painful and unpleasant. But there was something troubling apart from the pain, something that shouldn't have been. I put his silence down to disappointment with me, or that he was angry that I had not told him I was a virgin. God help the kind of girl I was.

I went to bed with him four times. The fourth time, and I guess I knew it from the first time, I paid for for many years after in some form or other, until Sarah Cameron, who said she slept with him for a year or three or four, told me that he had said the same thing to her, but she hadn't paid any attention to him. After I heard that things got better, although there were remainders for many years afterward. (I've forgotten what she did pay attention to or why she stopped seeing him.)

On that fourth night, Alex and I were smoking in his bed when he said, "I guess we ought to get up. Lou"—the young man with whom he shared a miserable ground floor on Jane Street—"will be coming home soon. Want a bath?"

It was a nasty little bathroom and I didn't like it. So I said, "No, thank you. I had one this morning."

"Did you?" he said. "Are you sure?"

Somewhere I began to tremble. Then I realized that I had always, in degrees, trembled in bed with him. But I had blamed myself: I was awkward, unadventurous, what an older generation called a stick-in-the-mud. (I've gone through my life blaming myself for almost anything that harmed me: what anybody did to me, what work failed, what meanness or malice was given, once the feeling against it had quieted, it was I who was the fool for not guessing it in time, for accepting lies I should have known to be lies, and so on. And what a puzzling mishmash that makes: because of course it always has some truth, and because of course it more often does not. It is vanity in the end, I guess, to think so much depends on you.)

"Are you very sure you had a bath this morning? Do try to remember because it may be of importance to your health."

I said I was absolutely sure, what did he mean?

He was out of bed now and had come around to sit next to me.

"Because," he said, "you always have an interesting but strange odor. So much depends on climate, doesn't it?"

They were marked years, the next one and the one after that. At a good and vigorous age, I couldn't go to bed with anybody with pleasure, without nerves and fear.

I never saw Alex again until about fifteen years later when I was crossing Fifth Avenue. He stopped to shake my hand, to tell me he was married, and that he and his wife had bought a farm. I have no memory of anything I said because I don't believe I said anything. I remember what I wanted to say, but I crossed the street and thought life has punished him, isn't that nice. The blond, boyish good looks had turned nasty and the malice showed hard now.

But I never knew about the word malice and Alex, never thought to use it about him, until a year or two after I was married. At that time my husband and I were living in a small Paris hotel room. One night we were talking about bathrooms, and he was telling me of the slum poverty of his childhood. The only privacy he had ever known was the dirty bathroom at the end of the hall, where the one toilet, the one cracked bath, was shared by six families. As a child, he would wait for the hour when all the neighbors would go to work. Then he would go there with a book – that being the only place to be alone – until somebody pounded on the door and cursed him.

I said, "You still spend a great deal of time in the bathroom."

"Habit. And that reminds me. Yesterday they were complaining downstairs that we use too much hot water."

"Can't beat the French for complaints," I said. "Aren't we entitled to one bath each a day?"

"In fairness," Arthur said, "for the price we pay I guess two would be O.K., but four is a lot."

"Four?" I said. "How do you get there?"

"You take three a day. You have ever since we've been married."

"You're a loony," I said. "I never take *three* baths."

"I've always meant to ask why you do that. When did it start? If you're working or busy or have fallen asleep you'll get up, just as if you weren't thinking about it, and take a third bath at three, or four o'clock in the morning. You often wake me, not knowing it, as if you were walking in your sleep."

It was too nuts, what he was saying, and I stared at him wondering why he talked that way. He was a kind man, he loved me, and he didn't make up things against me. And then I thought, but why do I think this is *against* me? Something is puzzling, out of order. That night, much later, after dinner, when we were sitting in the Dome for a coffee, I said, "Yes. It's true. About the three baths, but I've never known it until today. I wonder if I always did it."

The next day I wrote to my mother and asked her if I had been trained to take three baths a day and why? In the heat of New Orleans I could understand such a habit, but what about the many years after we had moved to New York? Two weeks later my mother sent her usual letter, but I guess she thought the bath question was a joke or she forgot it, which was in character.

The next few weeks I slept only a few hours a night. It was impossible to read by the dim bulb that hung in the center of the room. So the day following my mother's non-answer I decided to go to the phone office and call her in New York. But long distance calls were not usual then, and I knew that no matter what I said she would think I was sick or in trouble, so instead I sent off a night cable to my father saying we were fine but for literary reasons I wanted to know how long I had been taking baths three times a day, not to worry about my being crazy, just to cable back quick. He didn't cable, and I didn't blame him, but at the end of the week I had a note saying not all of my eccentricities were inherited, he had noticed the bath habit, but maybe just a year or so before I got married, and he had warned me that it was bad for the skin, and what literary purpose did I have in mind, he was anxious to read my adventures in hot water.

But nothing was funny to me in those weeks. I had cut the baths down to one a day and two over-zealous sponge baths for every curve and orifice. I thought of very little else except the bath stuff, certainly not work, or food, which I now barely ate. More puzzling, for the past three or four weeks, I had been refusing to sleep with my husband who didn't say anything, but I saw the puzzlement and the hurt it caused him. One night, immediately after I had said my kind of no, he turned his back to me.

I said, "It has nothing to do with you. It's me. I've only had one bath a day in the last few weeks. So I must smell. Do I smell?"

He turned over. "Do you *what?*"

"I think I smell and so you wouldn't like me."

"Why are you saying this? To save my feelings?"

"No. I'm telling you the truth."

"And you're crying," he said. "Go to sleep now and tell me about it when you're ready."

But I knew nothing to tell. That Sunday, when we usually took our picnic basket to Versailles, it rained and we stayed in our room. We tried to have our picnic there but I couldn't eat. I was always a thin young woman, but I knew I had lost too much weight and at dinner Arthur said, "What do you want to do? Maybe go home?"

"No. Look, I've kept many things from you but I don't mean to this time. I believe I smell and I can't stand it. I stop in the street to smell myself. I stand naked and smell myself. Yesterday in Le Printemps I almost asked a strange woman to smell me. I was halfway through the asking when I ran out. Maybe I am going crazy."

"I don't think you ever will," he said, "but I guess that doesn't help you now."

It was my generation in America, far behind Europe, who had begun to hear about Freud and analysts. We knew a few people who had gone to such doctors and we were respectful—which was more than people slightly older than we had been—but, I thought, I don't know where to find such a doctor and certainly I couldn't have paid him.

I had forty dollars from a short story I had just sold and Arthur gave me a hundred.

I chose a bargain ride to Lake Maggiore. I first stayed in a made-over servant's room in a fine hotel and then moved to a lovely room overlooking the lake in a small, cheaper hotel. At some place along the lake, or near it, I've forgotten, I made another hundred dollars at a gambling table in three nights, slept very late each day, took long walks, was severe about only one bath a day—except for one day when I cried all day and decided on three baths to shut myself up—and felt fine and wondered if denial was worth it, and denial of what and why? But the next day I was so ashamed of myself that I took no bath at all.

It was that night that I slept with an Englishman who was staying in the hotel with his wife and was very much into polo. I don't know why I slept with him because I didn't much like him. For a long time afterward, I told myself that I was testing myself on a man I didn't care about and who couldn't hurt me if he said anything about smelling. He didn't say anything except a lot of darlings and staged sexual groans.

It was all a comedy fake, which made me feel better, and before the couple left Maggiore I understood the reason: they thought I was rich and this was what he and she did for a living, how and why they moved around. I knew that because the husband and wife and I had a drink at the big hotel on the afternoon they were leaving—my treat—and Sarah came in with four or five people and sat down in a far corner. The Englishman said, "That's a beauty, that one. She's been here for weeks."

And his wife said in German, "That's the one you should have tried. She is easy, they say, and rich."

I must have laughed because my one-night lover asked me if Kober was a German name and I said that it was not. I stayed on for five more days, but I never saw Sarah at Maggiore again.

But the trip was O.K. I thought I was cured, owed the Englishman something. I went back to Paris, wrote a short story about the Englishman and his wife and me — nothing about the baths — sold it to an arty magazine for twenty dollars and believed I had recovered.

But recovery is not the word. You can't recover from what you do not understand. So, through the years, although the obsession had passed, I would wake up at odd hours of the night, heading for a bathtub, then making myself turn back for bed.

After I had gone to live with Dashiell Hammett, I used to take deep breaths when the bath stuff started and I would bury my face in the back of his neck until finally he would laugh and say he didn't mind my sniffing like a dog but did I know that the day before, with the Whittiers' three-month-old baby on my lap, I had sniffed the baby so much that Mary Whittier had said, "What are you looking for?" It had not occurred to me that the worry about how I smelled had broadened to where I was interested in how other people smelled. Then I asked the question I guess I had always wanted to ask.

I said to Hammett, "How do I smell to you? Nice or bad?"

"Nice."

"What does that mean?"

"It means nice."

"Nice doesn't mean anything. Tell me *how* I smell to you."

"I can't describe smells and I'm not going to try. Freud said something about that. You are off on one of your kicks and I'm sleepy."

So I guess the obsession never really disappeared until I saw Sarah again and for the life of me I cannot date that next meeting nor where it took place. I know only that she introduced me to her husband, Carter Cameron, who was a handsome young man from Chicago or Detroit or Cleveland, and that she and I found ourselves alone on a couch.

She said immediately, "I know people told you that I took Alex away from you. It isn't true."

"Nobody ever told me that, although Ferry hinted at it. But Ferry says anything that might cause a little trouble."

"I did sleep with him," she said, "for almost a year, I think. When I said I didn't want to marry him, guess what the stinker said: 'Jewish women take a ritual bath before a wedding ceremony. You are not a Jew but before you marry anybody you ought to learn from them because you have a very high odor in what is called your private parts.'"

I started to laugh, because my head was throbbing and I felt sickish. Then I stopped, to ask pardon for the laugh. I didn't need to: she was amused with my laugh, amused with the memory of Alex. I suddenly felt light and pleasant and grateful.

I said, "What was the matter with him? He said almost the same to me. Malice for all young girls?"

"I guess so. Or he tried for it. Anyway, he doesn't try anymore. He married a rich lesbian, I met her. And you don't tell her she smells because you don't come that close."

"Why did he marry her?"

"I don't know. Money, I think, but I don't know. Something else goes on with him. I'll be here for a few weeks. Let's have lunch on Tuesday. I'll call you Tuesday morning."

I was not to hear from Sarah again for many years. But I do know that her story of Alex did something very good for me, although I had a few odd minutes of wondering how she knew that I had ever slept with him.

Alex had told her, of course, the bastard. But something was wrong there because he was a secretive man, going to all measures to deceive, or, if that wasn't possible because of other people – it was almost never necessary — to whisper or cover his face if he was talking to you about nothing. I remember once bumping into him in a dentist's office when he had told me he was going to a Group Theatre rehearsal. Never mind. It was over for me, and I was grateful to Sarah. Placed, dated, over. I never went back to the excessive bathing, never thought about it or maybe only a few times in stress or trouble I couldn't place.

But it is a long jump from the years of worry to the day Sarah told me what Alex had said to her.

A couple of years after the dinner at "21" with Ferry and the dozing millionaire I was driving down from Boston and had decided to make a detour to see the lake where I had spent so many summers as a child and then as a very young girl in summer camp. I found the lake near Monterey, but the camp was gone although there were remains of a pier where I had once hit my head and sunk because I had never learned to make a shallow dive.

It was still lovely country and after I had taken a long walk, I drove on to Stockbridge where I had remembered a decent inn and restaurant. It wasn't there anymore, but a policeman told me about another place a few miles farther on. As I went to my room,

I heard a familiar voice on a hall phone, not familiar enough to stop me, but familiar enough somehow, somewhere, to keep me out of the dining room until as late as the rules allowed.

Ferry was sitting at a table alone. She jumped to her feet and pulled me to her table. Ferry always had an exhilarated manner, "peppy" was the term in those days. I wasn't in the mood for her or anybody else. I had spent the day thinking what I could bring back to memory's road from summers on the Monterey lake, where I had always felt lost, puzzled by everything I was doing and the kids I was doing them with, and yet each year, unprotesting, I allowed my parents to send me back. To what, for what, what could I have been about in those days? Now I wanted to learn something about myself, think about the years I had spent on the lake. I had counted on being alone.

I was annoyed at the interruption of Ferry and so I had a lot to drink that night, and a lot to eat. The talk from Ferry was new to me, odd, half-finished sentences, a break in the voice, references to things and places I didn't know about, sudden, sad, common reflections on "life" or "women and men." After dinner, which she insisted upon paying for, saying, "That's all I've got left, money. Makes me feel better to use it, better than you, I mean," we went along to her two rooms and she loaded a pipe with stuff I had never seen.

It was called marijuana, just that, in those days. I knew a few people who smoked it, but I was scared, the way many people used to alcohol are scared and snobbish about any other drug. It tasted good that night, I liked it, but it seemed to have no effect on me, although it certainly knocked over a few ash trays, and Ferry, or maybe it was the three martinis and the two brandies at dinner.

But long before the pipe was filled, and we were still on the Armagnac that Ferry dug from one of four Vuittons, I heard that the millionaire hubby-baby had had a crack-up from booze. Ferry, after consultation with his very rich mother – "a big, strong bitch who just looks wispy-poo and everybody believes her" – had brought him to Austen Riggs, a sanitarium in Stockbridge, mostly, in those days, available to boozers for drying out. Now, said Ferry, she was glad she had had the two abortions. A few minutes later she said she was sorry she hadn't had his children because she could have held Mama Biggy-poo up for real money. Ferry said, "But maybe I can still get pregnant. You know, if this joint allows him out for an afternoon or lets me in his room."

I said maybe it wouldn't take a whole afternoon, sometimes it doesn't, and Ferry said it was stuff like that that caused her not to like me and I said I didn't understand why she talked that way, so mean, and she began to cry.

It was like that most of the night. I didn't pass out until the light came up and I had gone outside for a look at the scenery, but I heard and said a lot of nut stuff. I don't like crying drunks, said so, I guess, and Ferry stopped crying and hissed at me and then crossed the room to kiss me and say something about such old friends and I said we were *not* old friends, we had not met until our twenties and then not seen each other more than ten times in the years afterward.

I think we both dozed off now and then, or Ferry talked on in a stream of my dozed, uncaring state or hers. I know only that the talk came in bursts of self-pity, a mention of immolation, then anger or bitterness, and that through it all I heard about the size of the millionaire's penis, not good, but maybe caused by mumps which Ferry knew his mother had arranged when he was a child. But he was a real sweet man, and kind, and she would not desert him, except for a few minutes later when she was bargaining with his mother for a divorce settlement, and why the hell had her father gone broke: she had only married to save her father and brothers and sisters, and somewhere I heard Alex mentioned several times, and somebody called Melanie. But I had gone outdoors, walked across a field, and passed out. I woke up in a blazing sun about a mile from the inn.

In those days there was only one standard remedy

for a hangover. My hangover had, by this time, on the wet grass, turned into shivers. I stumbled, half crawled back to my room, managed a shower, and sent for the remedy: a raw egg, a double sherry and two teaspoons of Worcestershire sauce. Then I slept for a few hours, heard the phone ringing and, several times, loud knocks on the door. When I woke up, I vomited, which is what the remedy was supposed to do if you were in good health. After you were sick the custom was to wait a while and then you drank a few beers which tasted fine and you could move for a few hours until it was time for a regular drink.

After two beers I went downstairs to check out and drive home. There was a note at the desk from Ferry. How could I have left her? Or had I? Please to come immediately, she had been to the nut joint and had awful news. She needed an old friend. . . . I paid my bill, got in the car and drove about five miles. It was not kindness that made me turn back. Something had stuck in my head through the fog-banks of the night before, something that had to do with me, something important I had missed.

Ferry was upstairs, sitting in a straight chair, holding a bath towel. This time it was not drink or grass, but big stuff, something I had never seen before.

It was to be, when Ferry reached middle age, a bad face, sharp and sly. But younger, although it was even then both sharp and sly, she was an attractive woman with a beautifully formed small body. Today, she was twenty years older than the night before.

She said, "They've done something to him. Please phone his ma to call the Detroit police. She bribes them enough. They'll come and get him fast. Her number is on the table."

I said, "What's the matter with you?"

She said, "Call his mama. The number is on the bed."

When she had repeated that twice again, I said no, I didn't think I should call his mama.

"He's been given something terrible, I tell you. They've given him something terrible. You know what he said? He said he didn't want me to come again. I was forbidden to visit him and he thought that was sensible. They've poisoned him with a drug. It's one of those places."

I said, "And what did they give you?"

"Are you crazy? Give me? I'm not a patient."

"Then you gave it to yourself?"

She got up, dropped the towel, and screamed, "You know nothing about anything. Now you deserve what you get. I've been nice to you—I was sleeping with Alex and he used to tell me about you. He wanted to *marry* me, and I wanted to marry him, but he was too poor."

"What did he tell you about me?"

"That you smelled. I mean down there and all over, too. *Smelled* and he couldn't stand it."

I said, "He was a shit made in Monel Metal. He also told Sarah she smelled."

Ferry stared at me and giggled. "You mean Melanie."

"Maybe there was a Melanie, but I never heard of her. I mean *Sarah*."

There was a long pause and then a large checkbook which had been on the table next to Ferry hit me in the head.

I said, "Stop that, you doped up fool."

She began to cry. I said, "And stop that, too."

There was sudden quiet. Ferry rearranged the towel to cover herself. She said in a tea party voice, "When you say Sarah do you mean Sarah?"

"I mean Sarah."

Ferry said, "I hear it all the time now. Her usual plots and schemes to fool other people. Her right name is Melaniess."

"Is it so bad not to want to be called Melaniess?"

"It is," said Ferry, "the denial of your parents."

I said, "There must be something wonderful about having been rich all your life. You can say any goddamn thing comes into your head. I've got to go now. If I can do anything for you except listen —"

The towel went as she sprang up, and so did the tea party voice. Rage or misery took over. For the next bad five minutes, the screams would go down to a whisper and sometimes I could not hear and sometimes I could not understand what she was saying. Ferry was pacing around me, speaking sometimes in a near howl with threats that didn't have anything to do with me. The talk seemed, at first, to do with Alex, but it settled, I think, on Sarah. Sarah, she said, had never even met Alex, never even *met* him, heard only about me and my smells from her, Ferry, in the days when she trusted Sarah, her playmate, her roommate at Foxcroft. She hated Sarah now and so would I if I only knew. And then came other accusations against Sarah, mostly about money and missing jewelry, but also about what Sarah had done to Ferry's life. Then she stumbled against the bed post and I had trouble pushing her onto the bed because she was shoving and kicking and crying all at the same time. After a few minutes—I do not know if she was asleep or simply quiet—I locked the two windows, unnecessary because the panes of glass in this fake Early American house were too small to fall through, locked her in her room, went down to the desk, handed the key to a young man and said Mrs. Lambert was ill, needed a doctor, would they call one, I would wait until he came. When the young man at the desk, looking bewildered, dialed a number, I went outside and drove away.

It is an April morning. I am on a tall ladder in the cow barn, with a large brush and a can of whitewash on a ledge of the ladder. Fred Herrmann, our young farmer — Hammett once said that Fred and I understood each other so well that, without discussion, we would, one night, both be found hanging together from a beam because we had not been able to sit down for three days and it was more restful to hang than to go to bed — was on a ladder at right angles, working on another wall of the barn.

I said, "Smells better already, doesn't it?"

"Yah," he said, still compromising between German and English. "But I like smell."

I said, "Not at the end of winter in the barn. All smells?"

We worked for ten or fifteen minutes without speaking.

"All smells?"

"What?" he asked.

"Do you like all smells?"

He laughed and went down the ladder for more paint.

I turned to watch him. "All smells? Do you like all smells?"

"All smells of animals," he said, "and I like very much manure."

"Smells from people?"

We had never, through the years, had any conversation like this, like anything but farm stuff or good-

natured, awkward Christmas dinners together sometimes.

"People? I do not smell people."

I had stopped working. I climbed down my ladder
and went outside to sit on an old broken piece of wall
and smoke a cigarette. I think I fell asleep because
I jumped when Fred's wife rang the cowbell for his
lunch. He and I walked toward his house together.

A few weeks later our three-year-old asparagus
plants began to come through the earth. We intended
to blanch them until we got the lovely white Belgian
kind that brought big money in the market. But Fred
and I had read different books on the blanching — a
whole row or individual plants covered with cheese-
cloth? — and we had spent the morning putting off
the decision. Fred was lying on the ground, his hand
testing the earth around the plant. Then he sniffed at
a clump and smiled.

"I like the smell," he said.

"Smell is strange, isn't it?" I said. "Sigmund Freud
said nobody could describe an odor, they just thought
they could."

"I don't believe that," he said. "I have many smells
from my childhood in Hamburg. My father's green-
house and others."

I said, "Do you like the smell of women?"

I cannot understand why I asked such a question. Certainly he was as shocked as I because he turned from lying on his stomach and stared up at me.

I felt awful, as if all of me was out of order and needed to go back into whatever semi-safe cage I had made around myself.

I began to lie. I said, "You see, we were having an argument the other night—" and then I moved away and walked fast back to the house.

I stayed away from Fred for the next few days. If he was working near the house, I made sure I was hidden by the kitchen porch or upstairs. The second or third day that I didn't go out of doors, Hammett said, "What's the matter with you? You're so nice and quiet."

"I did something I'm ashamed of, but I'm not going to tell you."

"I didn't ask you," he said, "and I've lived with you long enough to recognize the guilt periods. Has it ever occurred to you that your guilts might come from not wanting to think? Easy stuff."

I said, "I've heard that before about guilt and not thinking. I want to know something: do you like the smell of women?"

"Some, not all. Ask it flat."

"Do you like the smell of me?"

"You're some crazy lady," he said. "My bad luck."

Four or five years later I had a note from Ferry. It said that she was in New York for a few weeks staying at the Pierre and had bought herself a wonderful place in Montana. She said she had been shocked that I had not written her after Allen killed himself, but people were people and she'd like to see me, anyway.

I didn't answer that note, but a few days later I had a phone call from Ferry asking what had happened to me. I said not much. I was sorry about Allen's death. She said she was hurt that I hadn't written when he died, but people were people. I said they sure were. There was a kind of giggle and Ferry said, "Did you know Alex has written a book? It's got you in it and I thought you might want to do something about it just because, as we say in Montana, you sure don't come nicely and I guess a lot of people know your name now, and those awful Hollywood gossip people—"

I said, "You are a dear girl, Ferry, a dear girl."

She said thanks a couple of times and then there was a silence. Then I waited so long a time that she said there was no law about people writing books even if I didn't like what they said and before I was finished with whatever silliness there is to say to that, Ferry said, "I have told you over and over again that Sarah never told you the truth. She made all that up as she does everything, maybe even the baby she says she had."

I said, "If she invented Alex's saying she smelled, then she was being kind to me. And if he did tell her, she was being more than kind. Goodbye, Ferry, your mischief's too much for me."

Six months later I heard that Alex had published a novel and a few people told me I was in it, not good at all, but I never bought the novel and never let anybody tell me what Alex had said about me.

I said to Hammett, "You have a nice neck. It's so unexpected. Heavily corded and powerful and the rest of you is so thin and — "

On this particular night he had had to turn around because the strangest of our poodles, Meg, jumped on him and he moved because one had to be careful about what went on in Meg's head. He said, "Lilly, you've made that speech about my neck maybe fewer than a hundred times. It has never once occurred to you that telling a man his neck is fine and saying nothing about the rest of him might be tactless. I don't mind, but you're always wanting to know what is tact and what isn't."

"That isn't what I am talking about now," I said. "I only wanted to say that your neck always *smells* good. Don't *I* ever smell good?"

"Always," he said, "and silly, too, and that smell stuff has roots somewhere you ought to find out about or leave alone."

The next day I said, "My God, you're bright."

"Don't tell me about it," he said. "It'll be something like isn't it wonderful I open my pants to pee when lots of two-year-olds don't."

The piles and bundles and ribbons and rags turn into years, and then the years are gone. There is a light behind you certainly, but it is not bright enough to illuminate all of what you had hoped for. The light seems shadowed or masked with an unknown fabric. So much of what you had counted on as a solid wall of convictions now seems on bad nights, or in sickness, or just weakness, no longer made of much that can be leaned against. It is then that one can barely place oneself in time. All that you would swear had been, can only be found again if you have the energy to dig hard enough, and that is hard on the feet and the back, and sometimes you are frightened that near an edge is nothing. I guess that is what the Camerons are to me. Maybe that and other things, too.

But when was Sarah's shooting scandal? I do not know. Nor did I ever see it in a newspaper, although at least two or three people spoke as if they had seen it and thought it well known.

Certainly I know the so-called details of the story, but I am no longer sure whether all of them came from Sarah herself. I don't know how much was mishmash as told me, or if I half forgot and didn't even get it straight in the first place. I had no real information about Macpherson until Frank Costello told me about him a few years later.

When I first began to think about Sarah, I mean to think about writing about her, I wrote to a woman, an educated Czech lady, who had done research work for movies on which I had worked. I asked her if she'd do a job for me: would she find out when Sarah, whose name in those days had certainly been Cameron, had been involved in the Macpherson shootings in Los Angeles? She wrote back and said she had retired, didn't live in Los Angeles, but knew a splendid researcher. That gentleman wrote to me, asking for the years, and a few more facts, if I had them, and said the job would be easy. Six weeks later he wrote to say he could find nothing in the files of newspapers, except one item, and he was enclosing it.

The item is about two inches big. It says Macpherson's first name was Moses and, in parentheses, "Blazer," that the case brought against him for assault and attempted murder of Billy Martinelli had been dismissed.

I do not know if I saw Sarah that year, or a year later, or a few years later, and therefore I don't know when she told me about Macpherson.

But there are memories I have of her that I know to be accurate, although, as I have said before, I do not always know what she was saying or if what she said was sometimes based on her fantasies or the fantasies of others. I am certain, for example, what she said about Alex and the baby in the restaurant and so on.

And once, when we both were about twenty-five, I guess, we met in Small's in Harlem. I don't know who I was with but I know that she came in and sat at the next table with two men. She was in a beautiful loose dress with narrow shoulder straps that were too loose. She was moving to the music when the straps slipped and the top of the dress fell down. It was a fine sight: the beautiful breasts and the high loose piled fair hair. One of the men with her said, "You arrange things well."

Sarah said to me, "Why didn't you answer the invitation to my wedding? I only asked ten people."

"I never got it."

"Isn't that strange? Four of them didn't. Carter says I never sent them, but I did. I am sorry you weren't there. It was a good wedding. We meant it. Come and meet him tomorrow. I'll call you. He didn't want to come here tonight."

She didn't call. I was not to meet Carter Cameron for a long time. Later when I knew him and mentioned the period, he said he had been in a San Francisco hospital with a broken leg the night I saw Sarah at Small's. He said then, "The marriage had so much movement that I don't think she knew where I was. Usually Sarah didn't even want to go back to wherever we had left the valises."

And then there is nothing of Sarah until the morning I came into an enclosed garden at an inn on the Loire. I've been back to this inn so many times that I don't know what year that could have been.

I had had a good night. I was traveling with two people I liked very much — an old man and his physicist son. The son was my friend but his father had always interested me more and we had sat talking over a lot of wine until almost dawn. Then I had gone to my room, decided I was not sleepy and would spend the dawn watching for the boats that, in those days, and maybe even now, used to start down the river at the first light. But when I came out into the hotel's walled garden, the smell of a flower or a tree I couldn't recognize made me move away from the river seeking to identify the tree. For a while I followed a footpath in the woods. Then I found myself on a dirt road— I had long ago lost the smell—that I had never seen before and the double line of trees along it was so lovely that I followed it through the suddenly strong light and knew that I had been walking for a long time and had lost my way. I guess I walked for another half hour before I saw a roof in the distance to my right and I turned toward it to ask my way back. I had thought the house was closer to the road than it was because the line of trees continued up a fine driveway and through open iron gates. There was a small gate house and I knocked on the door, but nobody answered and when I looked through the window I saw that the room had no furniture. I went on around a long bend and stopped to look at a lovely pond whose other shore I could not see. It was so early in the morning that I thought it best to try to find the kitchen of the enormous chateau that after a few minutes came into view. I heard the sound of something—creaks or movements of some kind—and turned from the front of the house to the side, heading for the back, thinking it was logical the kitchen quarters were in the rear.

As I came around the side, I faced a large terrace. There were three people on the terrace: a man and two women. All three were in old-fashioned rocking chairs and obviously none of them had been speaking because I would have heard them. I coughed and said in my bad Louisiana French accent, "Pardon me. I am staying at the Auberge Charollais. I am lost. Would you allow me to call a taxi from the village?"

Sarah raised her head, put her finger to her mouth and said, "I will drive you back. Please wait a minute."

She went into the house and I looked at the man and woman. Both were in their middle thirties, I suppose, and both were startling in good looks. Neither said a word to me, and after a time that seemed so strange I backed away from the terrace and went to stand under a large honey locust.

It was a long wait and I grew so angry at the bad manners of the two on the terrace who ignored me standing awkward against a tree that I started down the drive. When I was near the gate Sarah, driving a very old open Rolls, stopped the car and opened the door.

She said, "I am sleepy." She yawned.

I said, "It is kind of you to drive me back."

She said, "We have been talking of the Paris flood all night."

"Has there been one since Thursday?"

"Oh, no. The one that came to Proust's door. Half of Paris was under water. The Gare Saint Lazare with bodies floating on the tracks and the Seine rushing with dead animals and people. They have a wonderful photograph—a young man, very beautiful, dead and still holding to his bullock. Wonderful for Proust, looking from his window, wasn't it?"

"If it was wonderful for Proust, then it was worth all the dead," I said.

"Don't you like Proust?"

I decided not to answer that but, after a few miles, in the lazy, sleepy voice that had always made me nervous, she repeated it. I said, "Crazy for the kid."

"What kid?"

"Kid Proust," I said. "Stop the junk, Sarah."

"What's your new husband's name?" she asked.

I said I had not married again.

"What about Vinnie?"

"Who is Vinnie?"

There was never to be an answer to that because we had gone perhaps fifty yards past the road to my hotel, and I knew the answer wouldn't matter, anyway.

"Let me out here, Sarah. This noisy piece of luxury car will wake the guests. And thank you."

As I opened the car door she said, "Ottoline will expect you for dinner. She'll send the car about nine. Will that do?"

"Ottoline who?"

"The woman on the terrace. She owns the joint.

She's the famous Ottoline Morrell and that's her
brother, or I guess he is. How is Vinnie?"

"I don't know," I said. Then realizing how irritable
my tone had been from the beginning and now knowing
why, I said, "How is your husband?"

She shrugged. "He isn't anymore."

"How is the boy?"

"Didn't you see him? He was on the terrace."

I said, "Sarah, my name is Lillian Hellman and
I thank you."

I walked back to the road that turned into the hotel.
The car had not passed me and so I looked back. It
was where I had left it, but Sarah had moved from
the seat at the wheel to the empty seat. Her body
was half turned, her head back on the seat. I guess
she was asleep.

Later in the day I asked the man who owned
the hotel—he had been telling me about the stage
experiences of his youth for perhaps the fourth time—
who were the people who owned the house where
I had found Sarah. He laughed and said that was the
great town mystery: it was owned by a German baron,
but the baron had only been there once as far as
anybody knew. It was occupied, when it was, by the
baron's friends or relatives, and only the gardeners
were local Frenchmen. All other top servants were
German, the bottom ones Spanish. The town disliked

all that because the German steward often made excursions to God knows where in Germany, returning with truckloads. No wine was ever bought in the town and seldom meat or cheese and often German fruit would be trucked down. *German* fruit. I asked about Ottoline Morrell but he had never heard the name.

Afraid that I would be telephoned for dinner, I went into the village in the late afternoon and ate my dinner there. But when I got back the only telephone call I had had was from Samuel Goldwyn in Hollywood to ask if I would call him back about picking up some shirts he had ordered in London.

It takes me a long time. I no longer know how many years went by, maybe until I read Bertrand Russell, before I knew that Lady Ottoline had been dead for at least ten years before that spring morning on the Loire terrace.

Why am I writing about Sarah? I really only began to think about her a few years ago, and then not often. Although I always rather liked her, she is of no importance to my life and never was. I do not know the truth about her or much of what I write here. It is the first time that has ever happened. It goes without saying that in their memoirs people should try to tell the truth as they see it or else what's the sense? Maybe time blurs or changes things for them. But you try, anyway. In the three memoir books I wrote, I tried very hard for the truth. I did try, but here I don't know much of what really happened and never tried to find out. In addition to the ordinary deceptions that you and others make in your life, time itself makes time fuzzy and meshes truth with half truth. But I can't seem to say it right. I am paying the penalty, I think, of a childish belief in absolutes, perhaps an equally childish rejection of them all. I guess I want to say how inattentive I was—most of us, I guess—to the whole damned stew. For example, how well I remember the name Morrell and the face of the girl on that terrace, and yet the years before and after Sarah on that day, what she told me and when, are all over the place, and except in a few places I can find no dates. When I talk to myself I can say it clear to me, about Sarah and other people, and places and dates, but I cannot seem to sort it out here. I am not alone: for years I have been amused or frightened or angry when people repeated or wrote stories about me, what I said or did. There have been few times when it was not somewhere inaccurate.

But it is not that I am inaccurate about Sarah: it's that I know so little about any of the Camerons. What I have written is the truth as I saw it, but the truth as I saw it, of course, doesn't have much to do with the truth. It's as if I have fitted parts of a picture

puzzle and then a child overturned it and threw out
some pieces.

I know I first heard the story of the "killing" and the
mess that supposedly followed when Hammett and I
were living in a good-looking rented house in Bel Air,
Los Angeles. I was working for Samuel Goldwyn but I
can't remember what Hammett was writing or doing
except drinking.

I know that I bumped into Sarah at a large Hollywood party and met her husband again, talked to him,
liked him. In those days, I liked too many people,
particularly anybody who was sober, because while I
was never as drunk as Hammett, I was learning fast.
Sarah's husband was still Carter Cameron. (Yes, she
had in France told me he was no longer her husband,
but he was.) He was a lawyer, somewhere along the
coast, not Los Angeles, or San Francisco. But time and
later events of that night made me forget whatever
else Carter Cameron told me about himself. Sarah and
Cameron and a large fat man, who I guess was a friend
of theirs, drove me home. Maybe I asked them in for
a drink, usual in those days, or they took for granted
they were expected to have one.

The house was fully lit, there was the sound of a
piano, and a woman was singing. I thought it was
a phonograph record until we came into the living

room. There was a small, good-looking woman at the piano. And I said hello and she nodded and I went off to get people drinks, helped by Cameron. When we came back, the lady was still playing and the fattish man and Sarah were sitting on opposite sides of the room. The man said, "Who is that?" pointing to the larger couch.

That was Hammett, passed out. I went over to shake him because I thought it polite, but knew he wouldn't come to for maybe twelve or fourteen hours because he didn't turn or frown and because in addition to whatever he had had to drink before he came home, there were six empty beer bottles and one third of a Scotch bottle on the floor next to him.

I sat down near the Camerons and the fat man said, "Who is she?"

I said to the woman at the piano, "Who are you, Madame?"

"I'm with him," she said, vaguely pointing to the couch. "Who are you?"

"I live here."

She laughed, "Not tonight."

"Why is that?" I asked.

"Because of him." She pointed to the sofa again, but she didn't know the room well enough to find it, so she pointed closer to the fat man.

"Who are you?" asked Sarah, turning to the fat man. "Do you know your name?"

Cameron said, "Sarah, I've told you three times that Phillips and I went to school together."

"I understand, old boy," said the man. "It's time I was beddie-bye in any case."

I don't any longer remember when he left, but I guess he must have at some point because a taxi came later for Sarah and Cameron. I was very occupied with Madame Piano. This was not the first time Hammett had brought ladies home, not having any intention of their staying—unless, of course, I was away, when he had moved two in for a week—but it was the first time a woman had faced me and had stayed on.

I said, "Knock off the piano playing, please."

She said, "You don't like music? I'm playing all the nice boys. Now just you all listen for a few minutes."

She was doing a medley of Kern and Gershwin and Berlin and now and then there would be something I had never heard—when it happened I consulted Sarah but she didn't know the song, either. After about ten minutes I had enough.

I said, "O.K. Thank you, very nice, but knock it off now for good."

"Don't you tell me what to do," she said. "Who the hell do you think you are?"

I said, "You're in my house, honey, and your escort

with whom I live, as they say, has passed out. He won't be in shape to take you home for another two days, maybe."

Three or four nights later I came home from the Goldwyn studio to find Sarah in the living room. Demerest, a fancy Negro, and his older lover, Carl, who was worth something, both of whom had worked for us for years, whispered at the door that a lady come along, but Demerest had not known what to say, and then, after more of the whispered stuff—he always whispered—I went past him. I was already irritable from a day with Sam Goldwyn and wasn't looking for visitors. Sarah was sitting in a very uncomfortable chair, looking whiter and more fragile than usual. She was holding a drink and said she was ready for another. Then Dash came home. He and I had been on most formal terms since the pass-out piano lady night, but before I could introduce them, Sarah said, "You are a very handsome man." Dash said, "Thank you ma'am" and smirked. This happened fairly often and always made me laugh. I laughed now with more malice than usual and he said, "You're having a good time with me these days, aren't you?"

Sarah said, "Last time I saw you, Mr. Hammett, you were on the couch and a lady friend was playing the piano to soothe you."

Hammett said, "So I've been told. But I don't remember it or her."

"And do not wish to be reminded," I said, "that I was forced to pop her to get her out of my bed and Carl had to drive her to whatever she calls home. Carl still has a bite on his hand. Think what you missed."

"Yes," Dash said.

I said, "But I think she loves you and she'll be back, don't you worry. The way they all do."

Dash told Sarah he hoped she would excuse him, he needed a bath and a long sleep "in what Lilly has come to call 'her' bed." He patted my head as he went toward the stairs and I said, "If you'll only give me the musician's phone number, I'll call her for you," and he disappeared.

Sarah said, "He has a nice nature. I am in trouble and need help."

The tale went in and out but I do not think I knew then when what she was describing had happened — a few days ago or a few months before. But it was not a question of memory: I was only half listening. There was no other way because there was no coherence. I had wanted to have my dinner alone — I was still very upset with Hammett and knew a change between us had to be faced — had been planning to drive out to Santa Monica, eat in a fish dump that used to be there, and walk on the sand.

But, through the hours with Sarah, I remember the word "purple" very well because it was said so often. Sarah had awakened in a purple room. Everything in it, including the piano, was a shade of purple. She was lying on the biggest couch she had ever seen, covered by a purple fur rug. She didn't recognize the room, didn't know how she got on the couch, didn't know how long she had been there. When she finally stood up, didn't understand why she was naked. She wrapped herself in a purple blanket "made of the skin of a purple tribe," looked around, heard voices coming somewhere off a terrace, heard the sound of a vacuum cleaner on her right. She went toward the vacuum cleaner, down a hall, to a very large bedroom, done entirely in eggplant, "which is, after all, another version of purple," and saw an old lady vacuuming a mattress. Vacuuming a mattress, said Sarah, was something she had never seen before. The lady paid no attention to Sarah, but Sarah thought it remarkable for so old a lady to lift a mattress and flip it to its other side as if it were a nightgown. Sarah said that when she knew the cleaning lady was going to pay her no mind, she said, "Could you tell me where my clothes are or a cup of coffee?"

The woman shut off the vacuum, said "What" in Italian and Sarah tried Italian. The woman pointed behind Sarah into a hall and went back to work.

Through stumbling into what somebody meant as a library and two other bedrooms, Sarah found a closet with a fur coat and a raincoat which was not hers and then the woman appeared with a pair of underpants, brown satin evening shoes, and a brown and gold chiffon dress.

Sarah said something about not wearing those in the daytime, but they were hers, she knew, and when she had put them on she went back for the raincoat, "very vulgar with silver mountings." She found the kitchen, was pouring herself a Scotch, had half drunk it, when the woman appeared again, took the bottle of Scotch from the counter, and handed Sarah a cup of excellent coffee.

The old lady said in English without an accent, "I will call a taxi. You wait downstairs." Sarah nodded and wandered back to the living room.

"I had to find out why I was there."

I was bored now. It all took too long to tell and I wanted to go out. Anyway it was not uncommon in those days to wake up in strange places, not knowing how you got there or what happened while you were there.

"Who I thanked," said Sarah.

"*Thanked?*" And I laughed.

"Don't you thank people when you don't know what you've done to them?"

"No. I'm usually worried about what they've done to me, or me to myself," and then I began to wonder what the hell *I* was doing in this conversation, why I was with Sarah at all.

"I heard voices from the terrace again. I went out there to look at those ridiculous things they plant so neither you nor they can move. One voice was loud and angry. That one said, 'Cross the room with nothing in your hands except the money and put it on this table.'

"Another voice waited for a long time and said, 'You know as well as I do, I don't keep money here. You'll get it Wednesday, as I told you. Now enough of this.' And I recognized that voice, but I had no name for it. You know what I mean?"

I did not know if I knew what she meant: I didn't want to make too many claims for my own messy and tipsy life. So I went on thinking about whether I knew what she meant and I missed the next part of what Sarah heard or saw from the terrace. When I caught up, she was standing close to the terrace wall, outside a kind of office where a handsome dark man was sitting at the desk. Two men, their backs turned to Sarah, were moving toward him. One of them had a gun in his hand and one of them had a gun hanging loosely at his side almost behind his leg.

The man with the showing gun said, "I told you for

the last time. Get up, open the safe, take out our money."

Either things became fuzzy for Sarah, nothing new, or for me, because I have never been clear about the order of the shots. There was one, I think Sarah said, and then the man at the desk, who had not had a gun, did have one, and he shot at the man who had done the talking. The second man ducked and shot at the man at the desk, and the man at the desk shot him through the desk's opening. The first man went down on his knees, shot again, but into a wall over the desk, and the other man fell over.

Sarah said the man at the desk said to her, "Glad you're here. Go and sit in the living room," and he turned back to his desk and picked up the phone.

Sarah said, "I seem to be in evening dress. There's a taxi waiting."

The man said, "Go sit down in the living room and don't worry about the taxi."

She went back to the living room and sat down because she was very tired. The old lady appeared and said, "Take off evening dress and button raincoat top to bottom."

Sarah said she told the lady she didn't like to be talked to that way, but she took off her dress. The old lady said, "Give shoes," and tore off Sarah's grandmother's wonderful cut steel buckles and gave her back the shoes.

Sarah said, "Those buckles are valuable," but the lady said, "Sit. I get you coffee. You need. Drink fast and much."

Sarah said, "Put a shot of brandy in it. That's what I need," and the woman, again without accent, said, "You need a hole in the head."

Long before this Sarah and I had gone to a hamburger joint on Sunset Boulevard. I was anxious to get her out of the house. Somewhere along in here a man and a woman stopped by the table and there was a lot of talk about horses, but Sarah didn't say a word to them and they went away. But their appearance had broken something, as plain narrative as Sarah was capable of, and she said things about what life did to memory, and she had lost the custody of her son, although Carter had given him back and supported her for a long time and I guess it was about then that it occurred to me that the shootings had not just happened yesterday or last week.

She stared at me. "Didn't you read about it?"

"No."

"That's strange. I was all over, all over. Society girl—I'm not, you know, Papa was an auto dealer in Mount Kisco—well, one photographer took a long chance. He ripped part of the raincoat before Macpherson hit him very hard and then I was half naked. I was asked about being the girl of a racketeer, and, you know, I guess I had been, although I'll never know." She smiled. "I've always thought that's the real wages of sin: you never get to know much."

"When did all this happen?"

"I don't know. I'm no good at dates. Right after that he went into big-time gambling."

"Who?"

"Mac Fadden. The man I've been talking about."

"He was Macpherson a minute ago."

"What difference does it make? But after that he went into big-time gambling. Clover Club. He owned it. You must have seen him there."

"When?"

"I don't know. Later. I saw you there or maybe heard about your being there then."

"He did not own it," I said, "and since Hammett and I went there almost every night, I'd have remembered him."

"You certainly would have. Whatever he did to me, he was the best looking thing I've ever seen."

I do not remember anything else we said. The whole tale began to be too strange with the claim that Macpherson owned the Clover Club. Anyway,

Sarah fell asleep in the restaurant and I had a hard time piling her into a taxi. I took her home to our guest room, slept on the couch, hoping Hammett would call for me, but he didn't. The next day was Sunday, too bad, and I didn't have to go to the studio, so for most of the day I had Sarah with more bits and pieces of her life and Som and the parade of years, and long silences and then sudden talk of the Macpherson trial, and a month spent in Algiers.

Maybe the strange mixture is why I don't remember very much. Or, as time and much of life has passed, my memory—which for the purpose of this tale has kept me awake sorting out what I am certain of, what maybe I added to what, because I didn't see or know the people—won't supply what I need to know.

But memory for us all is so nuts. Just last week I saw a man I once worked for. He had a large yacht in those days and a Scotch captain whose wife was traveling with him on that voyage. The captain didn't like the owner and the second day they had a loud fight. The captain had to win, of course, but when the boat returned to New York, the captain and his wife left, and the owner talked angrily about him and ingratitude and the rules of the sea for many years. That night, last week, I reminded the owner of the Scotch captain. He was amazed: he said he had never had a Scotch captain, there had never been a traveling wife on his boat, there had never been a fight. The other people at the table, if they were normal, must have thought I had some odd reason for my invention of the Scotchman, and in a little while I began to wonder if it had ever happened. It kept me awake that night. I got up very early and after missing the date of the boat trip by two years, I found the diary I had kept on that trip and clipped to the page was a post-card from the Scotch captain, sent the Christmas after the voyage, from Cornwall saying he and Betty had bought her great-uncle's house, liked Cornwall. The card said that each spring he picked any yacht he liked in the Mediterranean, and his wife sent her regrets for the nasty fight. I guess for everybody it goes like that, but you could easily go crazy and send others with you. It's no news that each of us has our own reasons for pretending, denying, affirming what was there and never there. And sometimes, of course, we have really forgotten. In my case, I have often forgotten what was important, what mattered to me most, what made me take an action that changed my life. And then, in time, people and reasons were lost in deep summer grass. I have tried to explain this, often to people who were hurt by my forgetfulness, but they do not understand, nor can I expect them to. It is not pleasant to be for-gotten. By now it doesn't worry me as much, but it has changed life and taken away parts of belief I would like to have back.

All of Sarah is like that for me, except the last time I know I saw her, which may be, or may not be, the last time most people saw her.

But I am still around the Macpherson time and the nights she told me about it and what she called the newspaper scandal that separated her, finally, from her husband and cost her custody of her son.

After she finished telling me about the scandal and how Macpherson now owned the Clover Club, which he didn't, I know we had lunch a few weeks later in the Goldwyn commissary and I took her over to where Jack Ford was shooting *The Hurricane.* So we were both fairly young that year, but not young enough for Sarah's "Do you find *any* of these men attractive, I mean in that way, enough to stick around for *five* minutes?"

In 1960, I was in Rome talking with William Wyler about the script of *The Children's Hour.* (In the censorship days of 1935 we had to change the story and the title and we had made *These Three*, a nice, modest picture that was based on the play.) Now Willy wanted to make the play as it had been written, but I did not want to go back to the past and was, in any case, working on something else. But we had agreed to two weeks of consultation about the script, and had chosen Rome—we were both in Europe on other errands— because in those days it was a lovely place to be. We each had a suite on the roof floor of the Hassler Hotel and, while a few other people often sunned themselves there, it was never crowded and the hotel had set up a table, a typewriter, and chairs in a special large T-shaped corner for us. I always woke up earlier than Willy and usually we quit work after lunch, went our own way, came together for a dinner work meeting. It was my habit, on good days, to eat my breakfast in our corner of the roof.

One Sunday it was as if the roof had just been discovered as the latest chic café. There had never been more than four or five people, often none at all, but now there must have been fifteen or twenty. There weren't many chairs so people had arranged themselves on the broad parapet. At first I thought they were all of one group. But I floundered around annoyed in my corner, waiting for Willy to plan a new place to work. I had carried a pot of coffee from my room and as I reached to pour myself a cup, idle about where things were, I dropped the pot, doing no damage but making a loud noise. Two or three groups looked up. One gentleman came to offer his aid. But nothing more had happened than some coffee had spilled on my shoes, and the pot was lying unharmed. The gentleman mopped my shoe with a napkin as I wiggled in discomfort at gallantry I was not used to. I thanked the gentleman too often, he kissed my hand and I watched him go back to his friends. The woman in the chair next to him had made almost a full turn to watch us and then a sudden turn back away from me, but not before I said in surprise, "Sarah!" Sarah paid no attention, turned to talk to a woman next to her. I thought she had not recognized me. When I decided to go back to my room I moved to pass the table where Sarah was sitting. I stopped, touched her shoulder.

"Sarah, I'm Lillian Hellman."

Sarah said, with a warm smile, "*Lei ha sbagliata, Signora, mi chiamo Signora Pinelli.*"

"That's fancier than Sarah Cameron," I said, and started to laugh. I don't know how many years since we had met, but she was still at the old loony stuff.

I had a friend in Rome who was a designer of textiles. I had told her I would like to buy a few presents to take home and that I liked old button sets. She took me to a charming small store where I was wandering around in the back, pleased with some lovely old nineteenth-century tassels. The owner and Janie were standing in the window so that he could reach for his best button sets.

Janie called back to me, "There's Sarah Cameron."

I turned, moved to the window, saw Sarah's back as she passed the shop.

"I know she's in Rome, but she didn't want to see me when I spoke to her a week ago."

Janie laughed. "When she first came here, she was stone broke. I asked her if she wanted a room for a few days with me. She stayed for two months. I didn't see much of her, but things got better for her some-where, somehow. Then, when I was in Milan for a week, she moved out. She had bought me a mink coat and removed the label, I guess, so I couldn't return it. There wasn't any question it was made for me because I am a tall woman. I've never heard from her since, although I wrote in care of Carter Cameron, hoping he would forward the letter."

"They've been divorced for a good many years."

Janie said, "I've seen her a few times since the mink coat. Once in a restaurant, once in a theatre, once walking down the Spanish steps.

"I said, 'Come and get the coat, Sarah. Your largesse is too great for a woman you do not wish to see.'

"She went by me without a word. There was some kind of small accident in the street and I lost her.

The second time I saw her was in the restaurant. I was with a few people, and so was she. Her pretense not to see me was so elaborate that I grew irrational. I almost pushed our table over getting to hers. I said, 'Sarah, send for the coat or tell me where to send it. It has never been worn. I will not wear the results of your doped up insanities.'

"A man next to Sarah got up. One of those men who pretend they are tall. He said, in very good English, 'Madame, there is a mistaken identity here.'"

"'The hell there is,' I said. 'Mind your business.'

"'I very much mind my business. You are addressing Signora Pinelli.'

"I started to laugh. Bad laugh, nasty, and I couldn't stop. Then, I think as the small-tall man was calling the head waiter, Sarah said in a silly German-Swedish-Finnish-Russian accent we had once invented in school, 'Life has turned out to be life, Janie. I meant you no harm.' I went back to my table. I've seen her a few times since, always with the tall-short man or alone, but we have never spoken again and I gave the coat to my sister."

Somewhere in the late 1930's, Lou Holtz, a funny stand-up comic in the old vaudeville and nightclub days, introduced me to Frank Costello. Costello didn't take any fancy to me as a woman, but I think I was the first literate one who had been offhand, had not slobbered over him, had not paid too much attention to who he was and didn't ask about rackets or murders. He sent flowers occasionally, and at Christmas a large hideous beaded evening bag, and took me to dinner at least once a month in a steak joint with fine pasta and puzzling Mouton-Rothschild. We didn't talk much, although many people came to the table, with short, almost nutty sentences, or stopped by to shake Frank's hand. As far as I can remember we never said a personal word, although somewhere I was told he lived in the West Fifties, had a wife, and I don't think any children. We would speak for three or four minutes and then not again for perhaps half an hour. I always had the hope that I would hear something wonderful, some secret that the papers didn't carry. But usually what talk we had at our awkward dinners was about books or movies or plays of five years ago. All of them best-sellers, almost never anything I had read or seen. I used to wonder why the books, in particular, interested Costello, where he had heard of them, or what life he saw in them. But I don't think he judged me for not knowing them: he was smart enough to guess he'd picked the wrong ones for high-toned talk with a writer lady. I guess they were comic dinners: I would wait eagerly for any small piece of information about a murder that might come from the plugged-in phone constantly brought to him, or the whispered messages from slick-looking men as they leaned into his ear, or handed over notes to him, but he never said more than yes or no to the phone or the men, and sometimes nothing at all. There were grunts into the phone, nods or shakes of the head to the over-shaved, over-perfumed who leaned in with messages. The notes would be burned in ash trays.

Once I made the mistake of telling him I liked Empire furniture and had just seen four chairs I would buy with my next Hollywood job. For at least three dinners, he asked me what Empire meant, when it had happened and could I buy him a book that showed what the Regency-Empire furniture looked like? I bought the book, told him he owed me forty dollars and he fetched a roll of bills which could have counted out to no less than four or five thousand dollars. The rest of that dinner was spent explaining why I could not take a five-hundred-dollar tip for all my trouble. After a while he said, "I guess I wouldn't take it, either, but then you and I are a lot alike."

It was that night, and for that answer, and because there was a woman in the restaurant who somehow reminded me of Sarah, that I asked what I had wanted to ask for a long time.

"Did you know a man called Macpherson who operated out of Los Angeles and shot two men? A woman I knew was in his apartment at the time and swore he shot in self-defense. So he never came to trial, or maybe he did, I'm not sure, but her testimony saved him."

Costello didn't answer me, so I began to invent what I didn't know. "She had a long affair with him, I guess, although he wasn't up her alley, I mean she was social, but she was a drinking girl and I guess he was very handsome and interesting."

Costello stared at me so sharply that I realized I had said something and I forgave myself fast for anything I might say before I had said it. "It wrecked her life. She had been married to a famous lawyer, a polo player" – I liked that bit – "and you know polo players do not forgive anything except horses, so he took the son away from her, and not even visiting rights, I think."

"You college kids," said Costello. "Polo. When was all that?"

I said, "I know about when she told it to me, but I'm not sure when it happened."

Costello said, "Macpherson was a third-rate runner. He once shot a sixteen-year-old punk in the foot for going through what he called his jewelry box. And in the years you got to be talking about, he was in his seventies. And I ain't no authority on what society girls think is handsome, but he was five feet six maybe, had a slashed nose and his face was all over slashed from the prison fights he'd been in all his life."

"But the purple penthouse," I said, "or maybe there was another Macpherson."

"There was no penthouse unless he borrowed it and nobody on earth would be ass enough to let him come in the door. There was another Macpherson, his brother, who died before you were born in a prize fight from a bad kidney blow because he tried to run."

I was shaking. None of my business, any of it, but I had believed it all for a long, long time. When Costello took me home he asked me what was the matter with me. I said that I was tired — this was the first full truth I had told all evening — I had been running around all day trying to collect money because many good folk had been trapped by the victorious Franco Fascists on the International Bridge from Spain to France, and had to be bribed off it or be killed or tortured. Hammett and I and many, many others had sent all the cash we had to Malraux, who would do the work of trying to bribe them out, but we hadn't yet collected enough money. When we reached my door, Costello took out the large roll of bills and handed me five thousand dollars. He said, "Friends of yours are friends of mine." During my gratitude speech I tried to explain about Spanish Republicans and Fascism. He said,

"None of that, please. Don't tell me about it. I don't get mixed up in politics and when you hand over the money, you forget my name, kid." I handed over the money the next morning and it was put down to "Anon" and I've never mentioned his contribution until now. But the grave's a fine and private place.

After thinking that I saw Sarah in the San Francisco hotel lobby, I never saw her again. I did have a letter from Ferry, who had married for the third time and was living in Dallas. She invited me to a New Year's Eve party to see her husband and at the end of the letter there was this sentence, "What do you know about Sarah's death? Like everything else wasn't it?" I had a shock when I first read the words and then I knew that Ferry never knew anything straight and she was really asking me for information or details. But I telephoned Dallas to say New Year's parties were not possible for me, what about Sarah's death, I hadn't heard of it.

Ferry said, "I thought *you* would know. There's a woman here, very high in museum circles, and her son went to school with Som. He bumped into Som who said his mother had died in Italy, her face all a mess,

in a bed with a dog and a child's teddy bear. I suppose
we should have guessed that."

I said that would have been a hard guess, who died
with a teddy bear, who did not, decided it was junk-
talk and said goodbye.

I have not meant to skip Carter Cameron, God knows.
But it's like the rest of all this, I do not know where
he belongs, or even if he belongs at all, or even when
I began to know him well. I most certainly remember years later when I met Cameron again. I knew,
of course, that he and Sarah had been divorced for
many years.

We met, I mean again, on an airplane when I was
going to see my beloved and very sick Aunt Hannah
in New Orleans. Cameron asked a man to change
seats with him and we sat next to each other, saying
very little throughout the ride, nothing of the past,
nothing of Sarah. He had been a remarkable-looking
young man, he was an even more remarkable-looking
man now.

When I came back to the hotel from my first visit to
my aunt in the hospital, there was a large amount of
flowers and an assortment of booze in my room with

a card from Cameron and soon after a telephone call from him, asking if I'd tell him where to find good gumbo and maybe come along and eat it with him. I knew a fine small Negro restaurant with real gumbo, but I was so moved by my visit to my aunt — my brave, sturdy, once so vigorous aunt — that I couldn't eat my gumbo and so Cameron ate it for me and took me home.

I remember telling him about my aunts — how one had died seven years before — and this one had never been sick and didn't know now why she was in a hospital, didn't know why I had come all the way to New Orleans, was worried to death that she couldn't pay the hospital bills and certainly wasn't going to let me do it for her. Then I started to cry at all these two fine ladies meant to me and now neither beloved woman would be here for me much longer, and I knew already the forever-deprivation of that.

Cameron came upstairs with me and I talked for a long time about my aunts: what they looked like, how they had lived doing the uncomplaining work of women brought up by middle-class intellectual parents who grew more educated as they grew poorer; going out to find any kind of work in a social class where that was a kind of disgrace; certainly pained by it once upon a time, but not by the time I knew them; proud, cranky, married to each other; frightened of life with brave faces; never owning anything that didn't come from sales or cheap auctions; cooking, scrubbing, never admitting a pain or an ache, so totally different from my mother's rich family—a comedy villain crew.

They were fine women for a little girl to be around although, of course, I didn't think of them that way when I was a child. But I did know from the time I was two or three years old that I enjoyed them. And, later on, I knew that the things I learned from them would be good and valuable for me all my life. Not that they were teachers, or ever tried to be teachers, but I guess that's what they were for me.

Somewhere children know true eccentrics from fake eccentrics, and even accept, with a little understanding, punishment from the real ones. My Aunt Hannah was overindulgent toward me, but my Aunt Jenny was not overindulgent toward anybody. She had a sharp tongue, was witty, and kind of good-natured irritable, when she wasn't furiously angry. Then the whole house would stop and all the boarders and servants would grow silent in fear of what she might say or do next. But she never did anything when she was very angry except to yell at a few people and to take a very hot bath. It was interesting, however, that almost everybody around her felt guilty when she was angry, and many people would try an apology for what they had not done. The only person who never apologized, because she quite correctly never felt guilty, was Carrie, the elderly Negro cook. They were quite a pair, my Aunt Jenny and Carrie. I don't know why they hated each other, but they did, and the kitchen was so politely conducted that one could feel the bristling anger behind the need for such comic good manners. Only once do I remember a real break between them. I wasn't in the house when that break came, so I don't know how and why it began. I know only that a dramatic announcement was made to the boarders at the dinner table that Carrie was no longer employed, and that for the next week the house would be in a disorganized state until my aunt could find an equal to Carrie. I do remember several imports arriving and departing, and then I remember, perhaps a month later, my aunt and I boarding two or three streetcars and getting transfers along the way, to a house in the Negro section that was called "Backertown." We walked for several blocks until we reached a small house where nobody answered the bell. We went up the steps and sat in two rocking chairs, and my aunt delivered herself of a rather angry denunciation of Carrie because she, my aunt, had given her the two rocking chairs as a Christmas present, and how ungrateful Carrie was to be using them now. And then suddenly Carrie appeared coming down the street, and my aunt got to her feet and almost stood at attention. When Carrie reached the fence, my aunt said, "I do not apologize. It is use-less to apologize. I will try to mend my ways."

Carrie said, "You won't mend your ways. You can't."

My aunt said, "I said I would try to mend my ways. I keep my word."

Carrie said, "Very well. I will return with you now. But get out of the rocking chair, you are too heavy a woman to be sitting in it. Go stand on the corner and wait for me."

I remember being very surprised at this exchange between them and even more surprised that my aunt did go and stand on the street corner with me, and we waited until Carrie had changed her clothes and joined us. I don't ever remember any further trouble through the years between Carrie and my aunt, although once Carrie said to me when I was about sixteen, "You sure got Miss Jenny's temper, and you sure better watch it. Things are getting more terrific in this country."

But the day we waited for Carrie on the street corner, I was impressed by Carrie. I had never seen anybody stand up to my Aunt Jenny before. But as the years went by, I realized that Carrie was a rather nasty woman, and I felt sorry for my proud aunt's depen-dence on this woman, who knew it and pushed her around because of it.

I think my aunt was in her late sixties when she decided that she was too old and felt too tired to go on with the boardinghouse. She called a council of her sister, Hannah, and my visiting mother and father and me to tell us that she was going to sell the house.

She said to my father, "I also have rheumatism. It runs in the family, I suppose, although I don't make as many complaints about it as some people I know."

"Perhaps," my father said, "because you are not in such great pain."

"Yes, of course," said my Aunt Jenny, "nobody has ever had the pains that you had during the one time that you were ever sick in your life."

By this time I was old enough to laugh at this reference to the long summer of my father's rheumatic attack. At that time, because he could not climb the steps to his bedroom, the so-called second sitting room-card room was cleaned out and, with great effort, was made into a fancy sickroom for him where all people were instructed to tiptoe past and never to enter without permission.

Without question, both my aunts were in love with their brother, and that summer was when I discovered it. Hannah, because of her job, was missing most of the day, but she now managed the long ride home for lunch, and returned an hour earlier than usual in the evening. I am told that the diet for rheumatism has now changed, but I am not sure that my father and his sisters didn't invent their own diet because it was entirely made up of things my father liked: there were sweetbreads under glass, and Hannah, on her way home for lunch, would go to a special French butcher for the finest of calf's liver. Jenny would trot off to the French market to buy turtle for the soup he wanted that was to be made only with vintage sherry, and to bribe one of the butchers to bribe his Cajun cousin to deliver the first of the wild ducks and the largest of the crayfish. Nothing but the best of champagne was brought into my father's room, and Jenny and Hannah had rather ugly little spats about who was to carry the trays, open the champagne. They were both extremely fond of my mother, but she was almost excluded from the room on the basis that she was too finely formed for the heaviness of the trays and too easily upset by my father's groans. But my father took pity on my mother's miserable outlander state and allowed her to read him the newspaper for an hour each day. I was about fifteen or sixteen at the time of this extraordinary performance and I knew perfectly well that he was only in half as much pain as the groans warranted. I made rather careful notes on what he did, because I was determined that I myself in some form would duplicate the illness in order to have the wonderful treats and the wonderful treatment.

Unfortunately, that time never came within the life of my aunts. In any case it was all good comedy except for the nasty Carrie, who one day said to me, "Miss Jenny and Miss Hannah been in love with your papa since the day he was in his cradle. Your mother been in love with him since the day she first laid eyes. Most women, I guess, though I sure don't know why."

But I knew why and I paid for it.

Ah, how much I had always wanted to be like my aunts and how much I feared being like them, on and on I went until Cameron put me on the bed and undressed me and found a box of aspirin. Then he rubbed my neck and I fell asleep on his shoulder.

We went out for breakfast. I went to the hospital. My aunt was sitting in a chair, neat and clean, listening to one of her three roommates telling the involved blood relationship she had to the new Queen of Carnival, high society stuff. I kissed my aunt's pretty straight brown hair and she asked me how I had done at school that day, and interrupted the social boasting of the Queen's relative in a most uncharacteristic way to explain that I hated tuna fish and peanut butter, always had, and wouldn't allow the cook to give me either for my school basket.

This had been true more than thirty years before, but I had forgotten how much it had amused Hannah what, as a small child, I would allow and what I wouldn't, and she, unlike other people, had thought it a mark of intelligence and splendid, emerging character. I said, hoping it would tell her that so many years had gone by, that I still disliked tuna, but I could go buy us something very nice for her hospital dinner. She said no, indeed, she'd be going home in a few hours, and I was to hurry back to school now, or they wouldn't like it and I would get bad marks.

In a little while, the doctor came in and asked me to wait for him outside. He came to sit by me and said he thought she was better off in the hospital, much cheaper than being cared for at home, and there probably wasn't long to go, but that he thought there was no sense my staying in New Orleans. Why didn't I telephone him every few days?

I couldn't bear to say goodbye to Hannah so I telephoned her lawyer, which is a funny way of saying it because neither aunt ever had a lawyer, never being in need of one, but this gent was the son of a famous man who when he first arrived in America from Germany, had slept on the porch of my grandfather's house because he didn't have any money and when he got rich and famous, he had always sent my aunts wonderful presents and begged to treat them to European trips that always ended with their allowing him to pay for three or four days in a cheap hotel in what was called "across the lake," a few miles from New Orleans. His son was a nice fellow and he said he knew Hannah had more money than she thought because he had handled her sister Jenny's will on her death, and I said never mind what she had, she didn't know it, and she was scared she could not pay the hospital bills, so I would pay them and he would tell her that they didn't cost much or anything else he thought was good for her. He said he loved her, too, and he would manage it all. I stopped by a travel agency to buy myself a ticket home.

I didn't see Cameron for a year, I guess, and I didn't write because I didn't know his address. But then he came to New York on a visit and in the next seven or eight years I guess I saw him maybe twenty or thirty times. Sometimes he would come to New York, once we sailed the Leeward Islands on a yawl he handled as simply and as well as he did everything, and once I went to visit him at his place. It was about a hundred miles north of San Francisco, wonderful land. The times we slept together were calm without passion, but it was, and is, one of the happy arrangements of my life. I guess that only means it was like almost everything else about this family: it had no meaning beyond the experience itself and even now I cannot find that, which is O.K., too, and maybe best.

Cameron and I liked each other, certainly, but that often makes people wait around hoping for more. We didn't talk about ourselves or the future. We felt no need for each other, but that isn't the way one usually wants things to go; parting, we never spoke of another meeting. Neither of us asked questions. I knew only that he had been a lawyer, didn't like it, had maybe enough money to buy himself this fine land and raise the Black Angus and cats and dogs and sheep he liked so much. It was an original house he had built for himself, and I think one of the reasons I liked it so much was because it had no sofas and there were beautiful pieces of old wood in desks and tables. I met only one friend—I am not sure he had any others. His friend was an elderly chemist who lived a piece down the road and who sang for us almost all night through a great deal of brandy and a thunderstorm.

I fell asleep from the brandy and when I woke up, Cameron was carrying me upstairs. We took showers, drank some beer, and were as sleepless as all such arrangements make you. I felt locked in, tender, and close to Cameron. Maybe it was why I made the mistake.

"Do you ever hear from Sarah or your son?"

"Don't do that," he said. He spoke very sharply and I was angry for a minute. Then I knew he was right and I went to sleep.

The next day we rode two large ponies to a beautiful, wide, fast stream I had never seen before.

"My God," he said, "you ride bad."

"I know. Maybe because my mother rode so well, raised on wild Alabama horses. She used to laugh at me on a horse, meaning no harm, but doing it anyway."

We had been in the cold stream for a long time and were lying now on hot grass when Cameron suddenly rose and hit each pony on the flank.

"They'll go home."

"You'd rather not see me fall off?"

"Yep," he said.

"She rode fine. She did most things fine, including thinking, although that would be hard for you to believe."

"You must have been very much in love."

"I don't know what you mean. She did think fine, but she hated that. God knows what caused it. Imagine *hating* to think, suspecting it, turning every way you could to drown it, I guess, or to prove something, but what?" Then, after a pause, "And to harm yourself along the way, and know it."

I didn't answer him. I didn't know what he was talking about and a guess would have been dangerous. After a while he went back into the stream and floated down a long way and swam back against a heavy current. I stopped. I think I was going to say something

unpleasant about Sarah and him. I wanted to but
I didn't.

On the walk home, he said, "You don't understand
what I mean about Sarah. No, it's not the way you
saw her."

I said, "Perhaps because I never really knew her or
wanted to. Maybe I'm jealous."

"You don't need to be," he said, "because I will
never love again. I am ashamed of the man who loved
Sarah and I won't have to do with him. She was a
brilliant girl. But I'm even more ashamed of loving
such a woman who made a nasty mess. First there
was some kind of mysticism, I guess. She would say
that nothing fit together, and nobody had ever made
it fit, and until it fit — so what was all the fuss about,
the thinking and the theories, and on and on and on.
That was hard to listen to but to try to answer —
I didn't like the doping that came later. It was mild
enough, I guess, when we left each other, but later
I heard it wasn't."

"Why did you give her custody of the boy?"

"I didn't. *She* gave *me* custody, without a fight. But
when Som was eleven he went to Rome on his yearly
visit to see his mother and wrote that he wanted to
live with her and never come back to me. I've seen
him once since then, God help me. Do you know why
he was called Som? Sarah insisted on it and when he

was six months old she said it meant 'the son of many.' "

I said, "My God!"

"It didn't matter. I knew she slept around. Unfortunately he is my son. He looks exactly like me."

I said, "Don't let's talk about Sarah again, only because I don't understand what you are talking about."

When we were almost at the house, he said, "O.K. I shouldn't have tried. Don't feel bad, don't try to understand. What I mean is my secret and I can't put it into words. It harmed me so much I don't think I can make sense about it or want to, really."

After that we were to see each other only once again and I am sorry for that because until that day it had been pleasant. After that day, it was something else, or would have been. I don't know. I don't know much about any of them. I mean I was uneasy: people who think they are telling you something, something large, and then can't, make me nervous.

About five or six years ago some friends of mine had a pretty daughter who was getting married. They were pleased that their daughter liked me and that I was their only older friend she asked to the wedding. My friends are rich people with a large Massachusetts estate. The groom, I take it, was a kind of itinerant musician, and the twenty or twenty-five wedding guests were what used to be known as hippies. It was good comedy that wedding: butlers and old family servants bustling, puzzled, frightened.

A charming small bridge over a stream had been draped with orchids for the ceremony. There was the pretty bride in a dress that looked like three dresses and maybe was; the bewildered but loyal parents; the minister who was simply known as a "cultist," although when I asked him later what cult, he said he didn't know what I meant. The cultist delivered a long series of marriage vows about vegetables merging into the male organ. Many people chimed into his sermon and soon all the words concerned the phallus, all in admiration of oneself or the promises of future admiration to others. The bride made a vow in poetic form unknown to me, but having to do with music and independence from marriage. The bridegroom took crumpled papers from his hot left hand and vowed *his* independence from marriage and somehow worked in the value of petunia salad. Every other line of his poem began with the word fucking, somehow looking down on it for reasons I didn't want to think about, but still promising "good procreations."

The bride's father was standing next to me and several times he turned and shrugged his shoulders at me.

Then, the ceremony over, a guitar began to play. It was immediately joined by four or five other guitars and singers. There was a little of early Dylan, the Beatles, but most of the stuff was original, I think. The originals picked up the theme of fucking, although occasionally they got into the dreams, the marvelous dreams of "true" human connection, or dope or God.

My feet began to hurt and I thought I would slip back to the house. I was standing near the back of the crowd, in a kind of second to last row of guests. It was no trouble to pat my host's arm and move past a girl. As I went a few steps past the last row a soft pleasant masculine voice said, "Fucking disturbs you? But not with my father?" I stopped walking, turned. Nobody had moved in the last row I had passed. Now, these years later, I wish, of course, I had left it all alone. That is a foolish regret because there was nothing I could do with the uproar that was happening to me. It was obvious that the voice had to have come from somebody near me; there had not been time for anybody to move very far. I went back to the last scraggly row where two guitarists were now at work. I moved back and forth along the last line of guests several times and, finding no clue, turned back toward the house. Then the young man made a mistake: *he* wanted to know where *I* was.

At the very edge of the group, moving away from a tree stump, was Carter Cameron's son. I have never before or after seen such a close resemblance between people; not even a Hollywood make-up man could have done such a job. I had known Boris Karloff very well: he was a good-looking man, and it had always seemed to me a miracle what they had done with his face for the Frankenstein movies. That was a minor job compared to what nature and life had done here: both Camerons were tall and the father had once been blond. The father's firm handsome features were here caved in, having been spoiled perhaps by Sarah's fine high cheek bones. One eyebrow had a burned scar above it and because the cheeks had caved the teeth seemed out of order, and maybe were. (I have never been sure of his teeth: maybe I only added their disorder to the horrid picture of the man's face later on.) The man was somewhere in his forties, but the face was of an old pervert waiting to be fixed in a funeral parlor. Certainly it was dope. But dope does not always cause such havoc. The havoc in his face and body was, to me, unidentifiable. I giggled because I was frightened.

"How is your mother?" I said.

"My father didn't tell you, or perhaps you're being cute?"

"I have not seen your father for several years and not many people have thought I was cute."

He did do something that maybe was a smile. "My father lost you once you found him out?"

I said, "I do not know what you're talking about. I like your father very much. We haven't seen each other because we live in different places. Goodbye."

I moved toward the house, away from him, I hoped. After a minute he caught up with me.

"You have not seen my father for several years. But you were sleeping with him long before that. My mother has been dead for eight years. It wasn't worth a mention to you? Do you find that O.K.?"

When I get angry, which has not been infrequent, I get cold and my skin becomes dry and crinkles. That was evidently happening now. Sometimes it has frightened people: it did not frighten Som.

He said, "You are thinking of hitting me. Don't do it. It would be dangerous."

"You are right. It would be dangerous. Say what you have to say and then move or I will call for help. They know me here very well, and my guess is that nobody here has ever seen you before."

I had made a good guess. His manner changed, his voice was less rasping, some small change took place.

"My mother was in hospital outside Florence. I phoned my father to ask him to come. He did not come. I phoned again, after she died, to ask if he wanted me to bring the body home. He said no, nor did he ever want me to phone him again. My mother died in poverty and I buried her in a pauper's grave. Bad stuff, eh?"

He watched me, then he moved off, going toward the long dirt road that led to the main road. I stayed around for an hour or so trying to find out if the parents of the bride knew him: they did not, nor did anybody they asked. Then I found the bride who had stopped singing and taken off a few dresses to dance with the groom. They didn't know him, they said, but they thought Ledbed Bergen did. I found Mr. Bergen, a guitarist, who said he had not brought him. He said Som always turned up at such occasions.

A week later I called Carter Cameron. A man said he was in New York and hung up before I could ask where. But I was rather glad of that because I did not know why I had telephoned.

A few mornings later, Cameron called me. I said I was leaving town for a week, which wasn't the truth, but after a half hour or so I called him back and said I could have dinner.

It was an odd meeting from the time he picked me up. I had gone downstairs ten minutes ahead of time, knowing I didn't want to give him a drink, wanting the anonymity of the lobby. But he must have wanted it too, because I saw him hold the taxi, not knowing I would be so available. We went to his usual expensive restaurant because he said, on the way, that he had been selling cattle for three days and needed something handsome to eat. I do not remember what we talked about over martinis but it was off balance, as had never happened before. It was as if we were trying to be new friends. We had a lot of good wine.

He said, "Why did you call me?"

"How did you know I did?"

"Because, my dopey, you told me."

But I had not. I said, "What difference does it make? Why haven't we called each other for two years?"

"Let's leave all that alone. It's nice to see you again, and that's enough."

In the next few minutes, as he was saying something or other, he stopped and said sharply, "What's the matter?"

I said, "A strange thing is happening to me. I can't see the other side of the room."

I rubbed my eyes and tried again. It was not a large restaurant, but I could not see anything farther than ten feet.

Carter said, "That sometimes happens when you have a headache."

"I haven't a headache. It will pass, I guess. But it's strange."

It was the first sign I was to have of the terrible eye trouble that came a year and a half later, although I have no proof that the night in the restaurant and the eye trouble are connected. I know only that when I report the incident to doctors they do not seem very interested or think it important. But it was the first time I remember thinking about my eyes or wondering if something was happening to me. I am no longer sure of what I felt that night. I do know that when we finally left the table I stumbled over the cord of our table lamp that all such upper class joints feel are needed, in imitation of nineteenth-century France.

But by that time I had other reasons for stumbling. I don't think I would ever have mentioned Som and thus nothing else would ever have been said or written if, in the middle of dinner, Cameron hadn't said, "I've bought a yawl. It's in Virgin Gorda. How about a week's sail? It would be good to be alone with you again."

The tone was so terrible. It was as if a bad actor had been given a line he did not like or understand. It was so false that I turned deliberately to stare at him. He stared back at me and then laughed.

"You caught me, yes?"

"What did you say it for? I've never done anything to you."

"But you might," he said, "you just might."

I said, as if a spring had gone loose, "I saw Som. I am sorry about Sarah's death, but what has a yawl got to do with things?"

Cameron said, "I haven't seen Som for many years and hope I never will again. But he wrote me that he saw you and told you about Sarah's death."

I said, "You haven't seen him for years, but he wrote you that he saw me. Strange. What for?"

"Don't waste your time figuring out Som's motives. They are very complex and often smart. A doctor I sent Som to, told me he was the only heroin taker he had ever met who controlled it exactly when he needed to and that made him dangerous. He does a nice little business flying around South America—nothing big time, but enough. Sometimes, many times, I've thought of killing him, but there'd be something odd about killing a man you haven't seen since he was a child, although I supported him until he was twenty-four."

"Did Sarah know about him?"

"Oh, sure, but she knew and saw things her way. I told you that before. She loved him, if Sarah's wandering-child's heart ever loved anything."

I said, "Did Som tell you she was sick?"

"No."

"Did you go to the funeral?"

Cameron laughed. "No."

I said, "It's silly to go to funerals unless your own feelings are —"

"Yes," he said. "It would have been particularly silly to go to Sarah's funeral because she didn't die."

After a while I said, "Then or now?"

"I don't know what that means."

I said, "Neither do I. How do you know she didn't die?"

"Because about two years ago she came to see me. She stayed for about an hour. It would have taken most women ten minutes to be more coherent, but Sarah was always a slow talker and thinks you know things you don't know. . . . It's a fairly simple case of fraud, although of course she doesn't think of it that way, and it's kind of funny, really, if you don't care about insurance companies, and I don't."

I said, "What happened?"

"I couldn't possibly know details from Sarah and, anyway, I had always suspected some hi-jinks. But I thought it was just as well I didn't know too much. Years before when she had money from someone or other, maybe even me, she had taken out a large insurance policy for Som. I guess he was in some kind of real trouble, or maybe they were just both bored. But then there came the time when the insurance money was remembered, needed, I guess. So they opened the recent coffin of a poverty peasant lady, put it back in place – I did not inquire about what they did with the dead lady, very probably smeared a little cash around – and a week later announced to the Florence papers that Sarah Cameron Petraccini something else or other had been killed in an auto accident, and the funeral had been in a Tuscan village. Sarah disappeared somewhere or other, many places, I suppose, for two or three years and everything was O.K. She moved, of course, under a false passport, and guess whose name she picked?"

After a minute, I said, "Alex's?"

"Who is Alex? Ferry's name. Rather witty, wasn't it? I think I told you we didn't have long together, Sarah and I."

"But why did Sarah come to see you, to tell you? You dislike the boy so much you would have seemed a dangerous man to tell – "

He coughed, drank a lot of water, said something about pepper, and said, "I've asked myself that many times. Sarah never has any reason, which is what makes her so remarkable. It was something Som had thought up. I'll probably wake up with a knife at my throat one morning."

I said, "You aren't frightened? She had some reason for coming and you know the reason."

He patted my hand. "You're in a bad humor. Have your eyes frightened you?"

"No."

He picked up my hand and kissed it. "You've been asking yourself all evening what you ever saw in me. That's happened to all of us. It's sad, isn't it?"

After a minute, I said, "I don't think that's what it is, but I guess it's something, but I don't know what it is and I'm sorry that it shows."

We left soon after that and had a cheerful enough conversation on the way home. I remember saying that the time I had seen Sarah in San Francisco seemed to coincide with the time she called on him. When we kissed at my door, he said, "If you ever find out what you felt tonight, would you drop me a note?"

I laughed. "I guess so."

At Martha's Vineyard a few months later I was eating the first corn I had planted. It was wonderful, unlike the two previous years. I had a fine bottle of wine and thought I put aside what I felt about a losing eye operation of a month before.

I decided to go for a swim. It had been at least a year since I had gone swimming alone, and I guess the wine made me feel capable, a long lost and long regretted feeling. I found our giant flashlight and walked the short path to the beach. It has been many years since I have had enough breath to swim for a long distance but a short swim is pleasant too and I am at home enough in the water to know I can turn over, float, and start again. The water was the right temperature, everything was good, everything was better; there was even the possibility that there could be some answer to the future and that it wouldn't be as bad as I had thought.

After a while, I turned over and started to swim toward what I thought was the shore. But I couldn't see the shore. The word frightened is not the word. I am not frightened in water. Something else was happening to me: I was collapsing in a way that had never happened before.

I knew I was near the breakwater because I could hear the water flapping against the rocks. I swam to it, and sat on one of the lower sharper rocks. I was in no danger. Too many boats had to come close to me as they slowed down in order to round the breakwater as they headed into the harbor.

I walked up the short path from the beach to my house. There is a giant rosa rugosa bush three or four feet off the path. I went off the path and fell into the bush. A rosa rugosa bush is not a good place to fall, the thorns are very bad, and I had fallen because I had forgotten to turn on the flashlight. But when I did, that was no excuse for bumping into the screen door of the kitchen and then burning myself in a hot bath that was supposed to clean the small, nasty, bleeding wounds from the bush. I lay down for a while and I guess I must have slept for a few minutes because when I woke up the world seemed gone. I was in the kind of temper that has no name because it is not temper but was some monumental despair that makes crazy people kill cats or stifle crying babies. I don't know. I went downstairs, made myself some coffee and drinking it I picked up a telephone.

I don't know why I chose Carter Cameron. But I sent this telegram to his telephone number, which is the only way to send it.

THERE ARE MISSING PIECES EVERYPLACE AND EVERYWHERE AND THEY ARE NOT MY BUSINESS UNLESS THEY TOUCH ME. BUT WHEN THEY TOUCH ME, I DO NOT WISH THEM TO BE BLACK. MY INSTINCT REPEAT INSTINCT REPEAT INSTINCT REPEAT INSTINCT IS THAT YOURS ARE BLACK. LILLIAN.

Two days later, Western Union called me to say that there was no Mr. Cameron at the telephone number on the telegram. I said there had to be, they said there wasn't. I dialed the California number and a man answered the phone. I asked for Carter Cameron.

The man said he didn't know Carter Cameron, he was a housepainter and was working in the house. I said the house belonged to Mr. Cameron. He said he'd never heard of Mr. Cameron. I said the house belonged to Mr. Cameron. He said he'd never heard of Mr. Cameron. I hung up.

Lillian Hellman was born in New Orleans, spent her childhood between New Orleans and New York, attended New York University and Columbia. In 1934 she launched her career as a playwright with *The Children's Hour*. Over the next three decades came a succession of major achievements in the theatre, among them *The Little Foxes*, *Watch on the Rhine*, *Another Part of the Forest*, *The Autumn Garden*, and *Toys in the Attic*. Miss Hellman has twice been the recipient of the New York Drama Critics Circle Award for the best play of the year (*Watch on the Rhine* and *Toys in the Attic*). In 1972 a definitive edition of all her work for the theatre was published as *The Collected Plays*.

Miss Hellman's memoir *An Unfinished Woman*, winner of the National Book Award, was published in 1969. It was followed in 1973 by *Pentimento* and in 1976 by *Scoundrel Time*. They were brought together in an omnibus volume with new commentaries by the author under the title *Three* in 1979.

Miss Hellman has received the Gold Medal for Drama from the National Institute of Arts and Letters, the Creative Arts Award from Brandeis University, and the MacDowell Award for outstanding contributions to the arts. She holds honorary degrees from Yale, Smith, Rutgers, and other universities. She has been Regents' Professor at the University of California in Berkeley, Distinguished Professor at Hunter College, and has taught at Harvard, Yale, and the Massachusetts Institute of Technology.